MIRACLES OF MEDICINE

ANTIBIOTICS

BY VIC KOVACS

 Gareth Stevens
PUBLISHING

Please visit our website, www.garethstevens.com.
For a free color catalog of all our high-quality books, call toll free 1-800-542-2595 or fax 1-877-542-2596.

Cataloging-in-Publication Data

Names: Kovacs, Vic.
Title: Antibiotics / Vic Kovacs.
Description: New York : Gareth Stevens Publishing, 2017. | Series: Miracles of medicine | Includes index.
Identifiers: ISBN 9781482461633 (pbk.) | ISBN 9781482461640 (library bound) |
    ISBN 9781482460957 (6 pack)
Subjects: LCSH: Antibiotics--Juvenile literature.
Classification: LCC RM267.K68 2017 | DDC 615.329--dc23

Published in 2017 by
Gareth Stevens Publishing
111 East 14th Street, Suite 349
New York, NY 10003

Developed and produced for Rosen by BlueAppleWorks Inc.

Managing Editor for BlueAppleWorks: Melissa McClellan
Designer: Joshua Avramson
Photo Research: Jane Reid
Editor: Marcia Abramson

Photo Credits: Cover Kateryna Kon/Shutterstock; Title page Kateryna Kon/Shutterstock; p. 5 Ricardo Tulio
Gandelman/Creative Commons; p. 6 Public Domain; p. 6 right, 8 Wellcome Images/Creative Commons; p. 7
Jan Verkolje/Public Domain; p. 9, 21 United Kingdom Government/Public Domain; p. 10 U.S. Army/Public
Domain; p. 11 National Institutes of Health/Public Domain; p. 13 Yoottana Tiyaworanan/Shutterstock; p. 14
Olha Rohulya/Shutterstock; p. 15 science photo/Shutterstock; p. 18 Austen Photography; p. 19 pittawut/
Shutterstock; p. 22, 24 Dmitry Kalinovsky/Shutterstock; p. 23 Akimov Igor/Shutterstock; p. 25 TRAIMAK/
Shutterstock; p. 27 Burlingham/Shutterstock; p. 29 Syda Productions/Shutterstock; p. 30 NEstudio/
Shutterstock; p. 31 Dragon Images/Shutterstock; p. 33 EPSTOCK/Shutterstock; p. 35 Dr Graham Beards/
Creative Commons; p. 36 Tyler Olson/Shutterstock; p. 37 kurhan/Shutterstock; p. 38 Kharkhan Oleg/
Shutterstock; p. 39 Marcin Balcerzak/Shutterstock; p. 41 Chatham House/Creative Commons

Printed in the United States of America
CPSIA compliance information: Batch CW17GS: For further information contact Gareth Stevens, New York, New York at 1-800-542-2595.

CONTENTS

CHAPTER 1

THE HISTORY OF ANTIBIOTICS

Bacteria are tiny living organisms, or microorganisms. They exist everywhere, and many are harmless, or even beneficial, to people. There are some bacteria that can invade the human body, causing **diseases** and other problems. A person can become infected by consuming contaminated food or water, by touching an infected person, by breathing the air an infected person has coughed or sneezed into or through a variety of other ways. Once a person is infected, the bacteria can cause illness through a few different means. Some bacteria simply multiply to the point that the host's system can't handle it. Others attack tissue head-on. Some even manufacture toxins that poison the infected person from inside their own body. Bacterial infections also vary based on their location.

ANTIBIOTIC POULTICES

IN ANCIENT JORDAN, A TYPE OF RED SOIL WAS USED TO TREAT SKIN INFECTIONS. RECENT STUDIES HAVE SHOWN THAT THIS SOIL ACTUALLY HAD ANTIBIOTIC BACTERIA IN IT. IN FACT, THE SOIL IS STILL USED BY SOME PEOPLE AS A TREATMENT THERE! ANCIENT EGYPTIANS USED MOLDY BREAD ON SKIN INFECTIONS, AND THE CHINESE DID THE SAME, BUT WITH TOFU!

PATHOGENIC BACTERIA

Many types of bacteria help with bodily functions, such as digestion, or at least do no harm. Pathogenic bacteria are the exception. These **pathogens** are responsible for deadly **maladies** including pneumonia, cholera, dysentery, typhoid fever, leprosy, plague, diphtheria and tuberculosis. Epidemics of these diseases have ravaged humanity since prehistoric times.

In the age of antibiotics and vaccinations, these diseases are no longer widespread, but they still break out in areas where people have less access to modern medicine. Even when antibiotics are available, pathogens can develop new ways to resist them. The bacteria that cause staph infections and tuberculosis, for example, have become more virulent and more resistant to treatment.

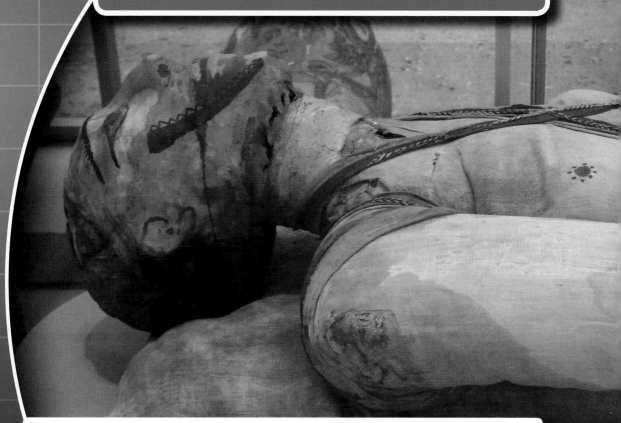

People have suffered for thousands of years from tuberculosis, a pathogenic bacterial infection that usually affects the lungs. Ancient Egyptian mummies show evidence of the disease, which still kills two to three million people each year.

Some affect wounds that haven't been cleaned or treated correctly. Others, like bacterial pneumonia, affect specific organs—in this case, the lungs. Common early symptoms of bacterial infections include fever, redness, swelling, and pain.

Infection has been a constant problem for humanity throughout history. Although ancient cultures weren't aware of **microbes** and how they caused disease, they certainly understood that people could get sick. Healers would observe the ill to try to learn how the sickness presented itself, and how it progressed. They also paid special attention to how the disease seemed to spread, as that would help them to prevent others from catching it. One early breakthrough was the observation that illness could be transmitted both by someone who was ill and by objects that person had been in contact with, such as clothes. Historical texts describe the symptoms of leprosy, an infection that, in later stages, can cause a person's fingers and toes to fall off. The same books also advise that people with the disease should be quarantined outside of the village to prevent its spread.

People with leprosy often had to wear special clothes and carry a warning bell or clapper (right), as depicted in this 15th century artwork.

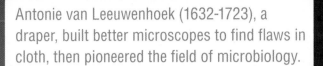

Antonie van Leeuwenhoek (1632-1723), a draper, built better microscopes to find flaws in cloth, then pioneered the field of microbiology.

Although people living in ancient times may not have known that tiny organisms were the reason people got sick, they did come up with some methods of protecting against and fighting infectious diseases.

A type of beer that was common in ancient Egypt, Jordan, and Nubia (part of modern Sudan) was high in streptomycetes, which is a bacteria that produce tetracycline. Tetracycline, which wasn't discovered until the 1940s, has antibiotic properties. Remaining records suggest that infectious diseases were rarer in the Nubian people than elsewhere in the ancient world.

Microbes weren't discovered until the 1670s, by a man named Antonie van Leeuwenhoek. A Dutchman, Leeuwenhoek made glass lenses, which he used to improve the microscopes of the time. Using these microscopes of his own design, he was the first person to actually see microbes such as bacteria. As with many innovations, Leeuwenhoek's discovery was not believed at first. His peers simply couldn't believe that such tiny living things existed! Eventually his discovery was accepted, but the abilities of microbes remained shrouded in mystery for many years.

It wasn't until the middle of the 19th century that scientists Louis Pasteur and Robert Koch proved that germ theory, hotly debated at the time, was true. Science finally understood that many diseases were caused by microbes such as bacteria and **viruses**.

With this discovery came the realization that if certain microbes could be stopped, so could the diseases they caused. One of the first scientists to harness this knowledge was a German doctor named Paul Ehrlich. In his research, he had noticed that some human-made dyes only colored certain microbes. He theorized that a medicine could be made that also only targeted microbes that caused disease. In 1909, he successfully developed a drug that killed off the bacteria that causes syphilis, while not harming the host. This was the first manufactured antimicrobial, and inspired much of the research that would come later.

One of the most important discoveries in medical history came about almost completely by accident. In September 1928, Alexander Fleming returned to his lab after a vacation. Before leaving, Fleming had been studying the bacteria staphylococci, which causes skin abscesses and other problems. Fleming wasn't known for his neatness, and he had left out several petri dishes.

Dr. Paul Ehrlich (1854-1915), a 1908 Nobel Prize recipient, made advances in immunology and invented the term "chemotherapy."

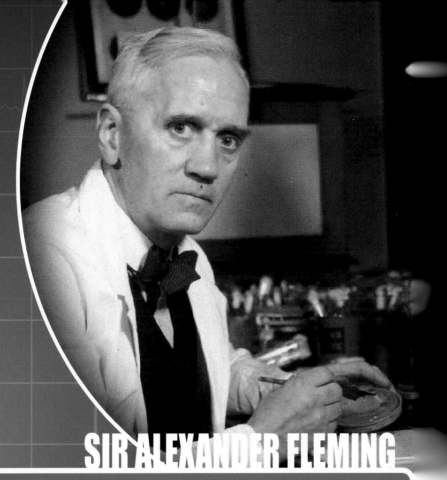

SIR ALEXANDER FLEMING

Born to Scottish farmers, Alexander Fleming (1881-1955) began his career as a shipping clerk. Upon inheriting some money from an uncle, he decided he'd rather try his hand at medicine. Graduating from medical school in 1906, he later obtained a specialized degree in the relatively new field of bacteriology. During World War I, he saw firsthand how deadly infected wounds could be. In his research, he found that the antiseptics used at the time to treat infections often did more harm than good. This inspired him to look into substances that could inhibit the growth of the bacteria. This work, combined with his inability to keep a tidy lab, would eventually lead to the discovery of penicillin, the first antibiotic, in 1928. For this immense contribution to medicine, he was knighted in 1944 and received a Nobel Prize in 1945.

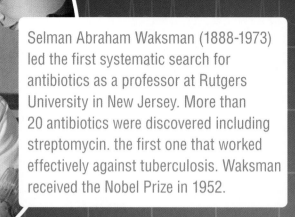

Selman Abraham Waksman (1888-1973) led the first systematic search for antibiotics as a professor at Rutgers University in New Jersey. More than 20 antibiotics were discovered including streptomycin. the first one that worked effectively against tuberculosis. Waksman received the Nobel Prize in 1952.

Fleming noticed that in one petri dish, a **mold** had started growing, and the bacteria wasn't growing around it.

Examining the mold, he realized it was penicillium, and found that it created a kind of "mold juice" that he called penicillin. Upon further study, he found that this mold juice could kill a variety of harmful bacteria. Unfortunately, his discovery wasn't given much attention by other scientists of the day. It wasn't until years later that a team from Oxford University realized the significance of Fleming's discovery and began researching and producing large quantities of penicillin, the world's first antibiotic. It saw heavy use during World War II, where it was used to cure infected wounds that would have been otherwise deadly.

Following the discovery and refinement of penicillin, there was a boom in research and development of new antibiotics. The 1940s alone saw the discovery of streptomycin, chloramphenicol, and tetracycline, among others. Streptomycin was actually the first to be discovered after penicillin, and one of its creators, Selman Waksman, is credited with coining the term "antibiotic" for popular use.

Penicillin saved many Allied soldiers from amputation and death during World War II.

WORKING DRUG

Alexander Fleming did not have enough financial support to turn his mold into a miracle drug. As World War II loomed, scientists Howard Florey and Ernst Chain led the Penicillin Project at Oxford University in England to rush its development. By May 1940, they had cured infected mice, which spurred U.S. drug companies as well as the U.S. and British governments to support their quest. Work shifted to the United States because England was being bombed by Germany. In Illinois, scientists learned to mass produce penicillin. Meanwhile, human testing proved that the new drug worked. By 1944, the project had produced 2.3 million doses of penicillin. Many people later considered penicillin a secret weapon that helped the Allies win the war, as Germany was able to produce only tiny amounts. Fleming, Chain, and Florey shared a Nobel Prize in 1945.

CLASSES OF ANTIBIOTICS

Antibiotics, sometimes known as antibacterials, are a type of drug that fights bacteria. There are many different kinds of antibiotics, but they can all be grouped into one of two types: bactericidal antibiotics and bacteriostatic antibiotics. Bactericidal antibiotics work by killing bacteria, while bacteriostatic antibiotics simply stop them from reproducing.

Along with this distinction, both types can be further divided into two additional groups: broad-spectrum antibiotics and narrow-spectrum antibiotics.

Broad-spectrum antibiotics are drugs that are effective at fighting a large number of different types of bacteria. Broad-spectrum antibiotics are effective if the patient is suffering from an infection where multiple types of bacteria are responsible.

FAST PROGRESS

IN 1907, ONLY ONE KIND OF ANTIBIOTIC WAS IN USE – ARSPHENAMINE, A TREATMENT FOR SYPHILIS. MANY CLASSES OF ANTIBIOTICS HAVE BEEN DISCOVERED SINCE THEN AND NOW THERE ARE THOUSANDS OF ANTIBIOTICS.

GENERIC AND BRAND NAMES

New antibiotics start with a chemical name that may be long and hard to say. The company that patents the drug gives it a shorter, catchier brand name. Eventually, other companies are allowed to make the drug under a generic name derived from the chemical name. Generics typically are less expensive but just as effective as name brands.

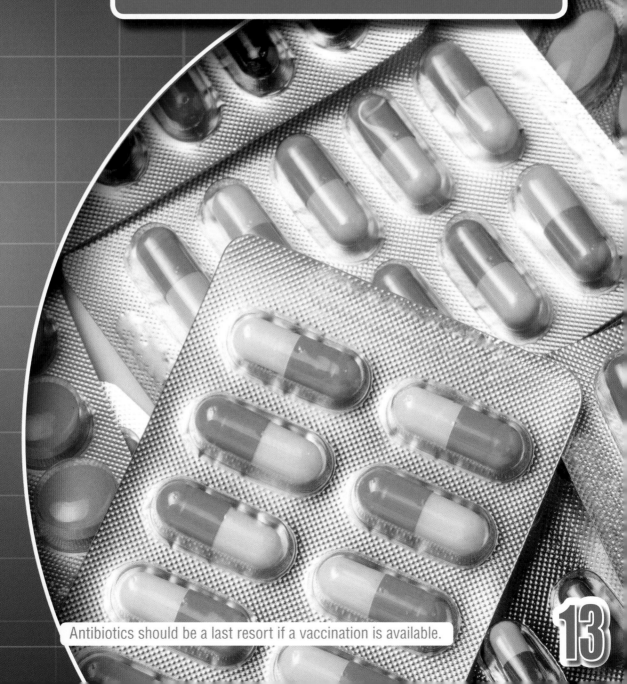

Antibiotics should be a last resort if a vaccination is available.

13

Narrow-spectrum antibiotics, on the other hand, only work against a few bacteria. Narrow-spectrum antibiotics are used when a specific type of bacteria has been identified as the cause of illness.

Doctors run blood tests to see if they think an illness will respond to a narrow-spectrum antibiotic. These drugs are used less often and so encounter less resistance from bacteria. If they don't work, though, a broad-spectrum antibiotic will be used instead.

BACTERICIDAL ANTIBIOTICS

A bactericidal antibiotic is a type of medicine that outright kills bacteria. Different antibiotics achieve this in different ways. Many antibiotics kill bacteria by impairing or preventing their ability to grow cell walls. This will lead to the bacteria eventually exploding. Drugs that function in this way include penicillins, cephalosporins, carbapenems, and monobactams.

Some antibiotics, such as fluoroquinolones, tamper with the bacteria's ability to make DNA. Unable to replicate, they then die out.

Others, like telithromycin, stop bacteria's ability to grow. When the antibiotic interrupts their ability to manufacture proteins they need to reach maturity, they simply wither away.

The fungus called penicillium chrysogenum is used to make broad-spectrum antibiotics. It is blue-green and likes cool temperatures.

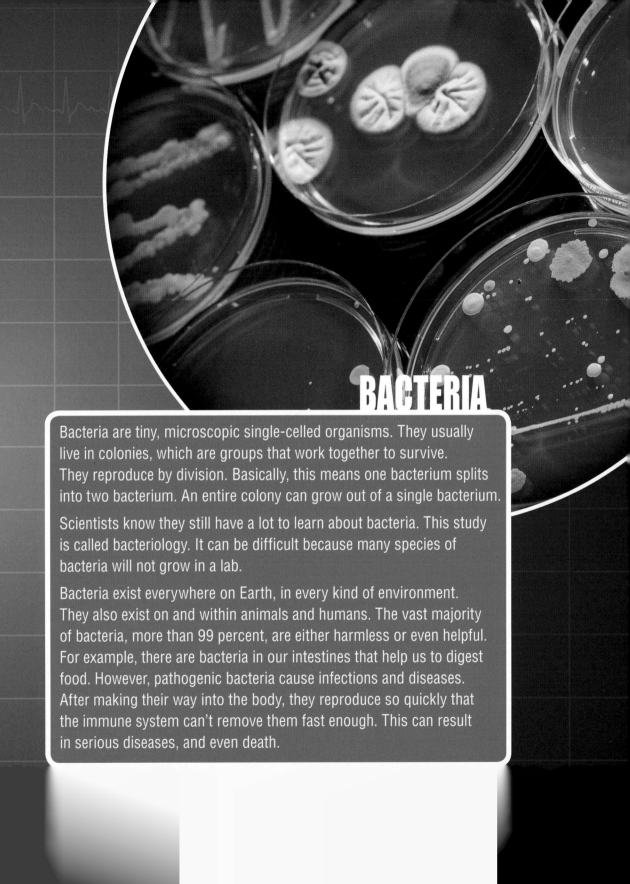

BACTERIA

Bacteria are tiny, microscopic single-celled organisms. They usually live in colonies, which are groups that work together to survive. They reproduce by division. Basically, this means one bacterium splits into two bacterium. An entire colony can grow out of a single bacterium.

Scientists know they still have a lot to learn about bacteria. This study is called bacteriology. It can be difficult because many species of bacteria will not grow in a lab.

Bacteria exist everywhere on Earth, in every kind of environment. They also exist on and within animals and humans. The vast majority of bacteria, more than 99 percent, are either harmless or even helpful. For example, there are bacteria in our intestines that help us to digest food. However, pathogenic bacteria cause infections and diseases. After making their way into the body, they reproduce so quickly that the immune system can't remove them fast enough. This can result in serious diseases, and even death.

BACTERIOSTATIC ANTIBIOTICS

Bacteriostatic antibiotics do not kill bacteria as bactericidal ones do. They simply stop bacteria from reproducing and multiplying, making them static. Once the bacteria are no longer reproducing and spreading, the body's immune system usually can take care of the infection. It formerly was believed that bacteriostatic antibiotics weren't as effective as bactericidal ones. However, some bacteriostatic drugs have been found to work as well in defeating certain infections as bactericidal agents. Some drugs are bacteriostatic in lower doses, and bactericidal in higher ones.

Like bactericidal antibiotics, there are a number of different kinds of bacteriostatic drugs that impede bacterial reproduction in different ways. Tetracyclines and macrolides interfere with protein formation, while others including sulfonamides disrupt their cellular processes.

A patient must continue to take bacteriostatic antibiotics while the immune system defeats the infection. Because these drugs do not kill the bacteria outright, if the patient stops taking them too soon, the bacteria can start reproducing again, and the infection can flare back up.

ANTIBIOTICS CLASSIFICATION

All the different antibiotics can be grouped into several large classes according to their chemical structure. Antibiotics in the same class work the same way and have similar effects on patients.

The main classes include:

- Penicillins and cephalosporins
- Fluoroquinolones
- Tetracyclines
- Macrolides
- Aminoglycosides

PENICILLINS

Penicillins, a bactericidal class of antibiotics, work by interfering with growth of the cell wall. One of the most common examples is amoxicillin, which children often take for strep or ear infections.

This class of drugs also is used widely to treat skin and dental infections, respiratory and urinary tract infections, and venereal diseases.

CEPHALOSPORINS

Cephalosporins, such as Keflex, have a similar structure to penicillin but were derived from a different fungus. They are used to treat the same ailments as well as staph infections.

FLUOROQUINOLONES

Fluoroquinolones, a bacteriocidal class of antibiotics, interfere with bacteria's DNA and reproduction. They are used when other antibiotics are not effective against bacterial bronchitis, sinusitis, urinary tract infections and certain other infections that spread rapidly in hospitals. A common example is Cipro, or ciprofloxacin.

TETRACYCLINES

Tetracyclines bind to the cell wall of bacteria and disrupt their ability to function. Since 1948, many types of this bacteriostatic antibiotic have been discovered. They work well against sinus and respiratory infections, ulcers, urinary and skin infections, Rocky Mountain spotted fever and typhoid.

Tetracyclines should not be taken by pregnant women or children under age 8 because they cause discoloration of developing teeth.

When tetracycline use discolors permanent teeth, dentists can correct the condition. Doctors still avoid using the drug in kids and pregnant women.

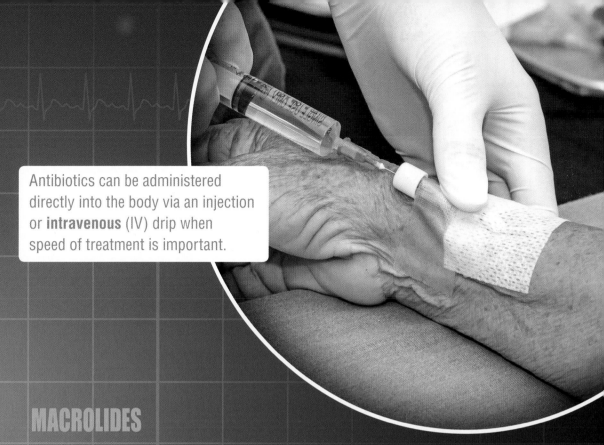

Antibiotics can be administered directly into the body via an injection or **intravenous** (IV) drip when speed of treatment is important.

MACROLIDES

Macrolides are bacteriostatic antibiotics that interfere with bacteria's ability to synthesize protein. They are used to treat cystic fibrosis and infections that don't respond well to other classes of antibiotic. Clarithromycin is a common example.

AMINOGLYCOSIDES

The aminoglycoside group also works by inhibiting protein synthesis among bacteria. Gentamicin is a common example. Aminoglycosides are generally used to treat complex and difficult infections, often in combination with penicillins or cephalosporins.

Aminoglycosides must be injected. They are potent and potentially dangerous, so patients are monitored carefully and usually take them only for a short time.

CHAPTER 3

PRODUCTION OF ANTIBIOTICS

There are a few steps that go into producing an antibiotic for commercial use. First, an antibiotic with the potential to be medically useful has to be identified. Because there are so many microbes, this is a big job. Identification usually takes place through a screening process. Microbes are grown and then tested against sample organisms to see if they have any effect. If they create a substance that damages the samples and aren't already known, they're studied further. However many that have an effect don't have an advantage over antibiotics already in use.

Next, further testing is done to determine how toxic the potential new antibiotic is and what benefits, exactly, it possesses. If an antibiotic is deemed suitable, it is then grown in large batches.

MAKING DO

DURING WORLD WAR II, WHEN THE FIRST LARGE BATCHES OF PENICILLIN WERE BEING MADE FOR ANIMAL TRIALS, THERE WAS A MATERIALS SHORTAGE. THIS LED TO A VARIETY OF UNUSUAL CONTAINERS LIKE BEDPANS AND BATHTUBS BEING JERRY-RIGGED TO GET THE JOB DONE!

Scientists have been searching for decades, but useful medicines have been developed from less than 1 percent of the antimicrobial agents they have found. Once an antibiotic reaches the stage of human trials, it still only has a 1 in 5 chance of becoming approved in the United States.

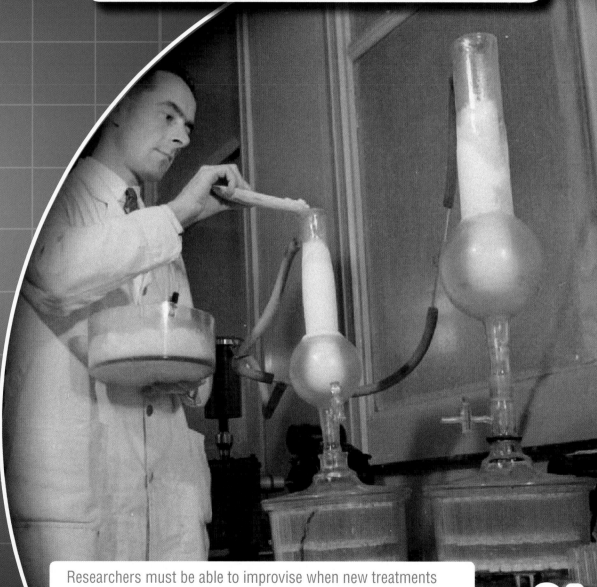

Researchers must be able to improvise when new treatments are needed quickly, as they did in World War II.

Once a potential antibiotic has been identified, large quantities must be made for testing and eventual public use. One common way to do this involves a process called fermentation.

During fermentation, the microorganism that produces the antibiotic is placed in huge containers along with a liquid, called a growth medium, that helps the organism to grow and reproduce. A number of factors are watched carefully to make sure the organism is growing as well as possible. Once enough of the organism has been grown, the actual antibiotic must be purified.

The types of microorganisms used in this process are rarely the same ones found in nature. They have usually been altered in some way to increase the amount of antibiotic that can be harvested from them. Some are deliberately mutated by exposing them to chemicals, X-rays, or other forms of radiation. Others are subject to a process called gene amplification, in which extra genes that make enzymes used in antibiotics are inserted into cells. These techniques allow these new microorganisms to produce larger amounts of antibiotics than they would naturally.

New technology helps scientists make breakthroughs in the development and production of antibiotics.

Fermentation does not happen overnight, but in several stages.

THE MANUFACTURING PROCESS

To make an antibiotic, the source microorganism must be isolated and then developed in sterile conditions with extreme care and precision to avoid contamination. It takes 5-8 days from the starter culture to shipment of the final product.

STARTING THE CULTURE

Obtaining a large, pure amount of the target organism is the first step in fermentation. A laboratory sample is put on a plate containing agar, a gel-like substance, to make a culture that is transferred to shake flasks where water and nutrients are added. The shake flasks, true to their name, stay in motion. This produces a suspension, which means that the microorganism and water don't combine but simply coexist.

The suspension goes into large containers called seed tanks along with everything it needs for growth. At the top of the list are purified water and a food source, such as molasses or soy meal, to provide sugar in the form of lactose or glucose. An ammonia salt provides nitrogen to help maintain metabolism. Just like people, antibiotics need trace elements, and these include phosphorus, sulfur, magnesium, zinc, iron, and copper, which are added as water-soluble salts. Finally, anti-foaming agents, such as lard oil or silicones, go into the mix. A pump delivers air that is **sterilized** and filtered so no impurities can get in, and mixers keep everything moving for 24 to 28 hours.

FERMENTATION

Now the mixture goes into giant fermentation tanks where the process continues on a much larger scale. These tanks can hold as much as 40,000 gallons (150,000 liters) of fluid. A constant water bath keeps the tank at about 77 degrees F (25 degrees C).

All of this gets the mix really cooking. To make sure everything is going well, small batches of the antibiotic broth are carefully extracted and tested along the way. Acids or bases may be added to keep the pH where it belongs.

The seed tanks are steel tanks designed to provide an ideal environment for growing microorganisms.

Once the fermentation stage is complete, the antibiotic powder is processed further and packaged into various usable forms.

ISOLATION AND PURIFICATION

Fermentation is considered complete after 3-5 days, when the mixture has produced the maximum amount of the antibiotic. Now the antibiotic must be isolated from the liquid and purified. Different methods are used, included specialized filters, centrifuges, and treatment with organic solvents. Whatever the method, the end product typically consists of antibiotic in a crystalline form that looks like a powder.

REFINING

The antibiotic powder goes through different manufacturing processes to turn it into usable medication. It can be put into capsules or pressed into tablets for adults, and made into flavored liquids or chewables for young children. For more serious cases, injections or IV drip bags are produced in order to get the medication into the bloodstream quickly.

For cuts and other skin ailments, antibiotics are put into ointments, sprays, and sometimes right onto the bandages sold in stores.

PACKAGING

Once in its final form, the antibiotic can be packaged, boxed, and shipped to hospitals, pharmacies, and medical offices. But first, logos and labels must be designed, printed, and attached to the packages along with dispensing and usage directions.

QUALITY CONTROL

In every step of this process, the antibiotic mixtures, flasks, tanks, separators and processing equipment must be kept sterile. Manufacturers typically perform a series of quality checks, especially during fermentation, to meet safety standards. In the United States, the Food and Drug Administration (FDA) oversees this process. In some cases, the FDA screens each batch of an antibiotic.

OTHER TECHNIQUES

Fermentation is not the only way to make antibiotics. Some are produced synthetically with laboratory chemicals. These may be combined with natural substances to form semi-synthetic antibiotics. Some synthetics and semi-synthetics have been found to work against strains of bacteria that are resistant to other antibiotics.

ALLERGIC REACTION

Some people might experience an allergic reaction to certain antibiotics. For example, penicillin allergies are somewhat common. Symptoms range from mild to severe, and can include redness, hives, and facial swelling. The most serious kind of allergic reaction is called anaphylaxis, and can cause breathing trouble, fainting, dizziness, and throat tightening. If any of these symptoms occur, the patient's doctor must be notified immediately so the patient can receive treatment and their **prescription** can be changed.

CHAPTER 4
USING ANTIBIOTICS

Antibiotics are used for treating bacterial infections. There are many types of antibiotics. Each works a little differently and acts on different types of bacteria. However they function, they're one of the most important weapons in humanity's fight against disease and illness.

Some antibiotics are used to treat specific infections. They're commonly used against ear infections, strep throat, urinary tract infections, and sinus infections. Antibiotics are also used to treat and prevent infected wounds. These can happen in cases where an injured part of the body was not cleaned properly, or if surgery was performed with tools that weren't properly sterilized.

Antibiotics are sometimes given to prevent infection before it can occur. For example, a course of antibiotics may be prescribed before a surgery or a major dental procedure. This is usually done in cases where the patient might have a compromised or suppressed immune system and be more susceptible to infection. One common example is cancer patients.

CAREFUL WITH ANTIBIOTICS!

NEVER STOP TAKING ANTIBIOTICS BECAUSE YOU FEEL BETTER. FOLLOW ALL THE DIRECTIONS TO MAKE SURE YOU STAY WELL. YOUR DOCTOR CHOSE THIS DRUG JUST FOR YOU AND JUST FOR THIS ILLNESS. DON'T SAVE IT FOR ANOTHER TIME OR SHARE IT WITH SOMEONE ELSE.

NOT TO FIGHT VIRUSES

Antibiotics are only effective in combating bacteria. They have no effect whatsoever on viruses. This is why antibiotics are never prescribed for the common cold or flu, since these illnesses are caused by viral infections. In fact, taking antibiotics for these ailments could even have harmful side effects.

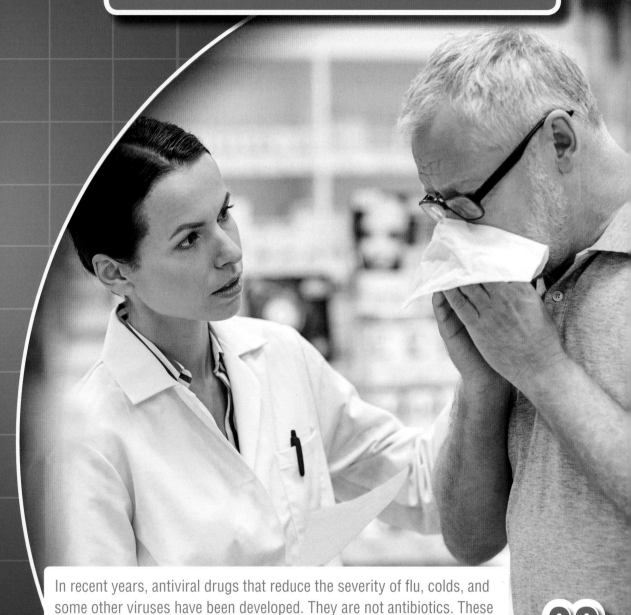

In recent years, antiviral drugs that reduce the severity of flu, colds, and some other viruses have been developed. They are not antibiotics. These prescription medications don't cure the virus but can speed up recovery.

ADMINISTRATION

Antibiotics can be taken in a few ways. The most common is orally, usually in pill form. These types of antibiotics are usually prescribed for mild to moderate infections, and can be taken by the patient without a doctor's supervision. In the case of more serious infections, injections or IV feeds are sometimes used.

Topical antibiotics are applied directly to the skin. They come in various formats including cream. spray, gel, powder, and ointment. Topical antibiotics help prevent infections caused by bacteria that get into minor cuts, scrapes, and burns. They are also used to treat severe acne. Treating minor wounds with antibiotics allows quicker healing. These kinds of antibiotics are effective, because they come into direct contact with the bacteria they're fighting. Most topical antibiotics do not require a prescription. Even so, they should be used only on the skin and for no more than five days. After that, it's time to visit the doctor for treatment of a stubborn problem.

First-aid products often combine one or more antibiotics to get a broad-spectrum effect. Triple antibiotic, one of the most popular topical products, contains neomycin, polymixin, and bacitracin.

Drug interactions can become a serious problem. To protect you, your doctor and pharmacist both need to know all the medicines and supplements you are taking. They also need to have your full health and allergy history.

EFFECTIVENESS

Antibiotics, like all drugs, are thoroughly tested for safety before they're approved for human consumption. However, side effects do sometimes occur. The most common are also the most mild, and include nausea, upset stomach, and soft stool (poop). More serious side effects include vomiting, diarrhea, difficulty breathing, rashes, and even fainting. Any of these symptoms should be immediately reported to a doctor.

Provided that an infection has been properly diagnosed, and the right antibiotic has been prescribed, antibiotics are generally effective. There are a few things that can interfere with them, though. The most important thing to do is to take antibiotics exactly as directed by your doctor. If they are supposed to be taken with a meal, don't take them on an empty stomach. Another common issue is that patients often don't take all of the antibiotics they have been prescribed. Once they begin feeling better, they assume they're cured and no longer need the medicine. This is especially dangerous when taking a bacteriostatic antibiotic, because the bacteria can begin reproducing again. This is why it's important to always follow a doctor's directions.

CHAPTER 5

RESISTANCE AND MISUSE

Since the discovery of penicillin, doctors and researchers have developed many more antibiotics. As antibiotics have become more common and widely used, bacteria have begun to develop immunity to them. This means that drugs that were once effective at treating an illness may no longer work. Today, science is racing to develop new drugs that can fight bacteria before they become invulnerable to treatment. There is a major danger that once treatable infections could again prove to be a serious threat to human beings.

DOMINO EFFECT

FARMERS OFTEN TREAT CROPS AND FOOD ANIMALS WITH ANTIBIOTICS TO MAKE THEM MORE PRODUCTIVE. WHEN THEY BECOME RESISTANT, A STRONGER ANTIBIOTIC IS USED. THESE ANTIBIOTICS GET INTO THE FOOD CHAIN, PUTTING OTHER ANIMALS AND PEOPLE AT RISK OF DEVELOPING RESISTANCE, TOO.

DANGERS OF MISUSE

Using unneeded antibiotics increases a person's chances of developing resistance to them. On top of that, once they are unleashed, antibiotic-resistant bacteria spread in the same ways as their more easily treated cousins.

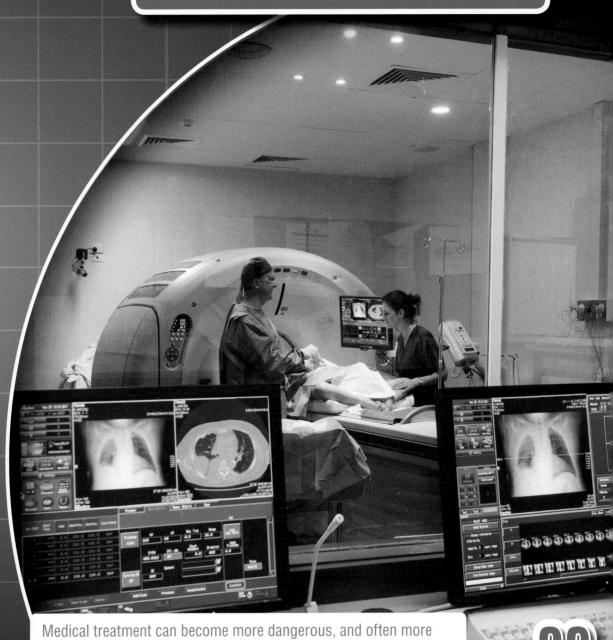

Medical treatment can become more dangerous, and often more expensive, when doctors must battle antibiotic-resistant microbes.

RESISTANCE

It's easy to forget that bacteria are living things, but they are. And, like all living things, they want to survive and reproduce. Bacteria that are resistant to antibiotics are more likely to achieve this.

Bacteria become resistant in one of two ways. The first is mutation. Mutation is a spontaneous change in the genetic material that makes up a bacterium, and it can have a variety of effects. Some of these mutations can make them immune to certain antibiotics. One mutation might allow the bacteria to create chemicals called enzymes. These enzymes then interact with the antibiotic in a way that renders it harmless. Another mutation might get rid of the part of the bacteria that the antibiotic targets. Some mutations strengthen the cell wall, keeping the antibiotic out, or create a kind of pump system that cycles the antibiotic through without reaching the bacterium's vulnerable part.

Bacteria can also pass resistance genes to other bacteria. Through a process called conjugation, a primitive type of mating, one bacterium is able to trade genetic material to another. This material can include genes that enable resistance to antibiotics. Viruses, which also infect bacteria, can also spread this genetic material between individual bacterium.

To test resistance, scientists infuse paper discs with antibiotics and place them on agar plates inoculated with bacteria. The antibiotics pictured on the left have done their work – the bacteria did not grow around them. In the dish on right, only three discs had much effect.

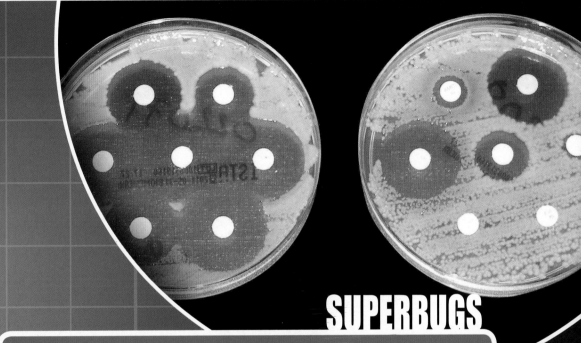

SUPERBUGS

Superbugs are strains of bacteria that have developed immunities after coming into contact with antibiotics, They cause life-threatening illnesses because they cannot be killed even with combinations of traditional antibiotics, although they may respond to new or seldom used antibiotic treatments.

Any species of bacteria has the potential to become a superbug. In 2013, the U.S. Centers for Disease Control counted at least 14 superbugs that posed a major threat to public health. About 2 million people battle a superbug every year, according to the CDC, and 23,000 die.

One well-known superbug is MRSA, a staph infection that spreads easily with skin contact. There are still antibiotics that work on MRSA, but scientists are concerned that could change.

Several types of bacteria have developed resistances to drugs. Staphylococcus aureus and Neisseria gonorrhoeae are both resistant to benzyl penicillin, a common cure.

Tuberculosis has also been developing immunity to drugs, with 1,042 resistant cases being recorded by the Centers for Disease Control in the U.S. in 2011. Food- and water-based infections such as salmonella and E. coli have also become more difficult to treat.

Hospitals, despite what you may think, are actually one of the top places people come into contact with resistant bacteria. With so many people being treated in such a small space, there are many opportunities for infection. Bacteria can be transferred by staff, contaminated equipment, or surfaces. The high use of antibiotics in hospitals can also lead to resistant strains emerging and infecting vulnerable patients in the same building. There are procedures in place to minimize this, and hospitals are mostly very good at preventing infections, but they're sadly not perfect.

Hospitals and nursing homes can become breeding grounds for drug-resistant bacteria because people who are ill have lowered resistance.

Although antibiotics can't help with flu or colds, many people still want their doctors to prescribe them, and many doctors still do. Studies have found that as many as half of all antibiotic prescriptions are not needed.

TOO MANY PRESCRIPTIONS

The main reason so many bacteria have developed resistance to drugs is misuse of antibiotics. This happens in a variety of ways. One common occurrence is people who request antibiotics for viral infections, such as a cold or flu. Because an antibiotic has no effect on viruses, not only does it have no effect on their illness, but it can also lead to antibiotic resistance. Some people are given the wrong prescription, which has the same effect. Others who are given the correct prescription use it in the wrong way.

People might stop taking their antibiotics as soon as they feel better, but before the bacteria colony has actually been eliminated. Or they might do the opposite, and take it for too long. Even taking too low a dose can help bacteria to develop a resistance. This is because, if patients take antibiotics incorrectly, resistant bacteria have a chance to overtake the unresistant in the population. The chances of this happening also increase the more they're exposed to antibiotics.

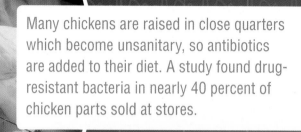

Many chickens are raised in close quarters which become unsanitary, so antibiotics are added to their diet. A study found drug-resistant bacteria in nearly 40 percent of chicken parts sold at stores.

ANTIBIOTIC USE IN AGRICULTURE

Agricultural use of antibiotics accounts for about 50 percent of total use, at least within the U.S. This has led to its own host of issues. Part of the reason for such a high rate of use is that they're not just given as medicine. Antibiotics are used to help animals grow bigger much faster than normal. This allows farmers to maximize their profits, as it takes less time to grow enough meat to be lucrative. Unfortunately, this over-reliance on antibiotics can lead to resistance, and there is evidence that this resistance can even be passed on to humans. As a result, farmers are being encouraged to cut down on how many antibiotics they give their **livestock**. At the grocery store, antibiotic-free meat has become an increasingly popular option for consumers concerned about these issues.

Antibiotic residue has also been found in crops. Vegetables including corn and potatoes that are fertilized with manure from animals given antibiotics have shown traces of the drugs. The manure contaminates the soil crops are grown in, and can lead to greater antibacterial resistance in the general environment. Once in soil, antibiotics can even leak into nearby water sources.

Antibiotics are invaluable tools for promoting health and wellness in both humans and animals. But they must be used properly, and in moderation, to maintain their effectiveness. If overuse and misuse continues, humanity could see a major resurgence in once minor and treatable infections. The rise in drug-resistant strains of bacteria cannot be ignored, and must be dealt with swiftly.

Some countries in Europe have passed laws to remove antibiotics from animal feed and placed other restrictions on their use in livestock. This will likely become more common in the future, as antibiotic resistance becomes an even bigger problem throughout the world.

Agricultural and environmental scientists monitor corn and other crops to determine what level of antibiotics they contain.

CHAPTER 6

ANTIBIOTICS OF THE FUTURE

Antibiotic resistance is a major issue. At some point, bacteria will become immune to all drugs that are available at present. This is why it's of the utmost importance that both new antibiotics and new types of antibiotics are in constant development. If this problem is ignored, humanity will be vulnerable to all kinds of dangerous and deadly diseases and infections.

Some scientists are searching for new antibiotics in previously untapped ares. Instead of soil, where naturally occurring antibiotics have traditionally been found, they're looking in other places, such as bodies of water. Others are looking within animals and plants.

Research is also being done into alternate methods of battling bacteria. One promising treatment is called phage therapy. This uses bacteriophages, which are viruses that feed on a specific strain of bacteria. So the proper bacteriophage will just get rid of bad bacteria causing an infection, and not the body's good bacteria.

This means they have fewer side effects than broad-spectrum antibiotics. Phage resistance does eventually happen, but phages, like other viruses, mutate constantly to remain effective.

SERIOUS TROUBLE

The World Health Organization (WHO) warns that drug-resistant pathogens have become a serious concern. "We are on the brink of losing these miracle cures," WHO Director-General Dr. Margaret Chan said in a 2011 statement. "In the absence of urgent corrective and protective actions, the world is heading towards a post-antibiotic era, in which many common infections will no longer have a cure and, once again, kill unabated." What can be done? WHO asks everyone, from individuals to agribusinesses to government, to use existing antibiotics wisely and support major efforts to develop new ones.

Dr. Margaret Chan, a Chinese-Canadian public health specialist, was elected by WHO as director-general through 2017. She is known for managing epidemics of avian flu and SARS in Hong Kong.

Presently, antibiotics target one of five parts of a bacterium: cell walls, cell membranes, proteins, genetic material, or metabolism. Scientists are trying to find alternate targets, or a way to make antibiotics target more than one thing at a time. That way, if the bacteria develops a resistance by, say, fortifying its cell wall, its proteins would still be vulnerable to attack. It would be much harder for bacteria to develop multiple resistances at once.

Vaccines are another avenue that might lead to decreased reliance on antibiotics. Vaccines give a person immunity to specific types of bacteria and viruses by triggering an immune response in the body. The immune system then manufactures antibodies to fight off that infection. Many diseases that are caused by bacteria already have vaccines to prevent them. If others can be developed, there will be fewer bacterial infections, and less of a need to treat them with antibiotics.

Some scientists are looking into compounds that might modify bacteria's resistance to antibiotics. One example is efflux inhibitors. Efflux systems are what allow bacteria to move antibiotics out of the cell. If a substance that stops that mechanism from working could be found, antibiotics that have ceased working could once again be made effective against certain bacteria.

WHAT CAN I DO?

Scientists and researchers are working tirelessly to develop new antibiotics and new ways to combat bacteria. There are also a number of things ordinary people can do to help reduce the need for them. Using antibiotics correctly is a huge one. Unnecessary prescriptions need to be eliminated, and necessary ones must be used as directed by a doctor.

Proper sanitation is also an easy way to cut down on possible infections. Wash your hands after going to the bathroom, after coughing or sneezing, before and after preparing and eating food, and in any other situation where bacteria could be transmitted. However, there's an increasing amount of evidence that you shouldn't use antibacterial soaps when washing your hands. They're not particularly more effective than regular soaps, but they can lead to increased antibacterial resistance. So, there's no real reward, but there is the potential to create massive harm. This is also an issue with other products such as household cleaners, laundry detergent, and even mattresses. Remember, there's good bacteria and bad bacteria, and trying to wipe all of it out eventually just makes it stronger.

The mass production of antibiotics has only been happening since the 20th century. As important as research into new antibiotics is, it is also hugely important to remember to use the ones we have already responsibly. After all, if we don't, the war between disease-causing microbes and human beings might not end the way we want it to.

TIMELINE OF ANTIBIOTIC DISCOVERIES

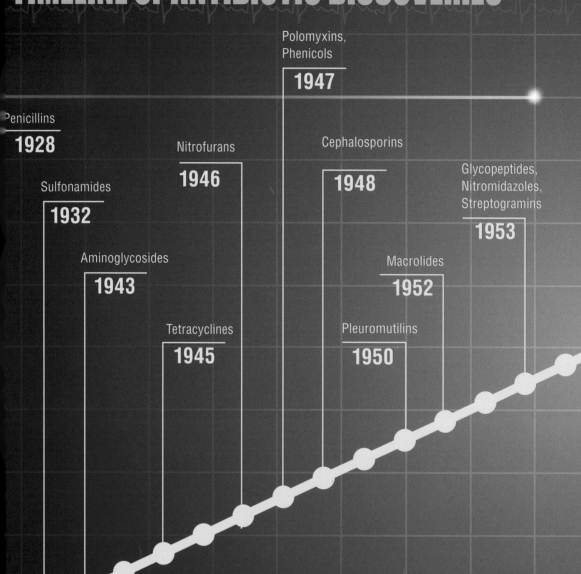

Polomyxins,
Phenicols
1947

Penicillins
1928

Nitrofurans
1946

Cephalosporins
1948

Glycopeptides,
Nitromidazoles,
Streptogramins
1953

Sulfonamides
1932

Aminoglycosides
1943

Macrolides
1952

Tetracyclines
1945

Pleuromutilins
1950

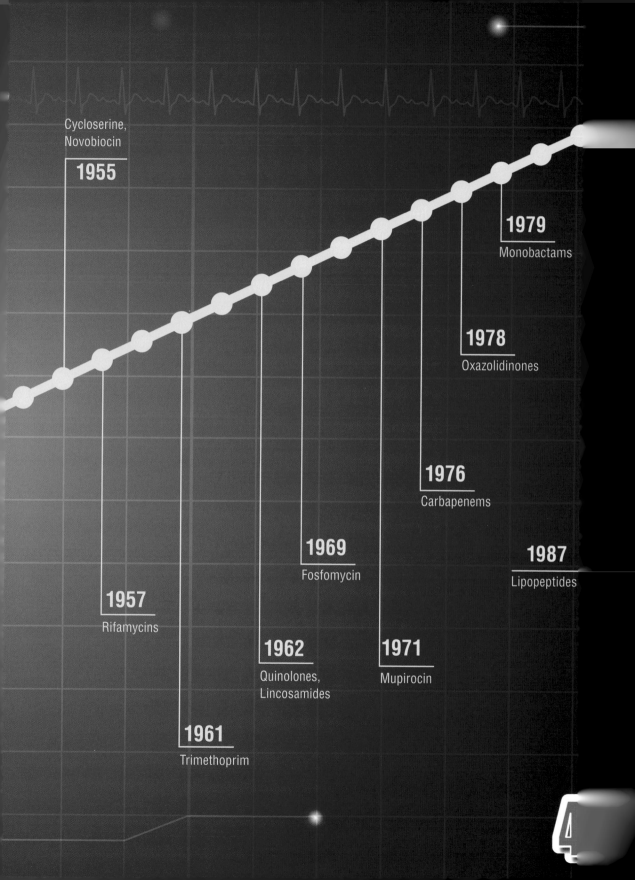

GLOSSARY

bacteria: Single-celled organisms that are rod, spiral, or sphere shaped, some of which can cause disease.

disease: A condition that affects living things and prevents them from functioning as well as they're normally able to.

intravenous: Entering the body through a vein; a name for a type of therapy.

livestock: Tame animals raised on farms and similar places for a variety of purposes including food and labor.

maladies: Ailments or diseases.

microbes: Microscopic organisms including bacteria, as well as some fungi, algae, and tiny animals.

mold: A type of fungus that grows in the shape of filaments, and often contributes to the breakdown of organic matter.

pathogen: A type of bacteria, virus, fungus, or other microorganism that causes disease.

prescription: A written order made by a doctor to provide a patient with a specific type of medicine.

sterilized: Having been cleaned to the point of being free from bacteria and other microorganisms.

virus: Tiny parasites that can only replicate in living cells of other organisms. Too small to be seen with a microscope, they can infect anything, from humans all the way down to a single bacterium.

FOR MORE INFORMATION

BOOKS

Rooney, Anne. *You Wouldn't Want to Live Without Antibiotics*
Danbury, CT: Franklin Watts, 2014.

Williams, Mary E. *Antibiotics*.
San Diego, CA: Greenhaven Press, 2014.

Zuchora-Walske, Christine. *Antibiotics*.
Edina, MN: ABDO Publishing Company, 2013.

WEBSITES

www.cdc.gov/drugresistance/
Centers for Disease Control and Prevention section about antibiotics and antimicrobial resistance.

www.kids.frontiersin.org/
Frontiers for Young Minds is a nonprofit scientific journal written for kids by scientists.

INDEX